The Super School Brand

Peter Kibe Ngugi

BlueRose ONE.com
Stories Matter
NewDelhi • London

BLUEROSE PUBLISHERS
India | U.K.

For permissions requests or inquiries regarding this publication, please contact:

BLUEROSE PUBLISHERS
www.BlueRoseONE.com
info@bluerosepublishers.com
+91 8882 898 898
+4407342408967

ISBN: 978-93-7310-461-4

Cover design: Aman Sharma
Typesetting: Manisha Rawat

First Edition: November 2025

Dedication

To my dear wife Catherine, who has always stood with me through every storm in the thick and thin of hailstones. You have ardently stuck by me; at all times with unwavering love and strength like a colossus.

A reputable high end school brand in Kenya.

Source: https://images.app.goo.gl/2pAYx2MVZTAn7W7K9

Preface

This book on school branding is intended to provide school managers with an array of great ideas on how to give their schools a stunning new look! That ragged school image and a stale reputation can be expunged to give your school a refreshing new look and a trendy name. Effective branding will rekindle customers' interest in your institution and its educational products and services.

Marketers say that your brand is your identity. A popular brand means happy customers. Developing a unique and recognizable identity serve to make your organization, products and services stand out. A strong identity help organizations to align with the market place, attract investment, motivate employees and gratify external stakeholders.

Studies on corporate communication in schools have shown that there is a significant relationship between the strength of organization identity and stakeholder happiness. Marketing communication tools transmit your brand assets to your target audience with the aim of creating the best organization identity. This organizational identity is basically expressed through the four branding elements namely: visual markers, management behavior, corporate culture and marketing communication.

Branding is a strategic management function mainly performed by principals and school boards. My experience in schools has discovered a gap in school branding materials. This has prompted me to prepare this guide on how schools can be rebranded to turn them into more reputable institutions. The time to re-brand your school to outshine your competitors is now! The book has captioned some examples of local and international super brands just to stir up your imagination. You can take more time to study them in details.

TABLE OF CONTENTS

CHAPTER 1
INTRODUCTION

This chapter introduces the concept of corporate branding and its benefits. The study on branding elements and assets will help the reader to apply the ideas easily and practically in his re-branding process to create that Super School which you desire. Later, we shall delve deep into school branding.

WHAT IS BRANDING?

Corporate brands are marks denoting ownership, image-building devices and symbols associated with the key organizational values. Generally speaking, branding is the use of advertising, design and other methods to make people recognize and remember your organization as a distinct product. Branding is thus the image formation process: the way corporate values and personalities are translated into an organization identity, leading to the formation of an ideally favorable image, reputation, which in turn, results into creating a competitive advantage.

The purpose of branding is to establish a favorable reputation with an organization's stakeholders which in turn makes such stakeholders buy that organization's products and services, to work for or to invest in that organization. Companies construct brand identities as a conduit through which pleasurable experiences are consumed by their stakeholders.

The most obvious way of recognizing corporate identity is through visual marks and advertisement. Every organization is unique and its identity is found on the organization's own roots, its personality, its strengths and its weaknesses. The identity of the corporation must be so clear that it becomes the yardstick against which its products and services, behavior and action are measured. The identity cannot be simply a slogan, a collection of phrases: it must be visible, tangible and all embracing and touching the very core of its existence. Everything that the organization does must be an affirmation of its identity.

Corporate identity answer questions like "Who are we as a company?" and "Where do we want to go?" Identities are pre-conceived, then consciously and strategically created but at times they are caused by accidental and stimulus reaction. Organizational identity consists of current practices, history, values and behavior emanating from inside the organization from internal stakeholders. It is the actual, positive or negative perception expressed as "Who or what do we believe we are?"

BENEFITS OF BRANDING

Identity is now widely recognized as an effective strategic instrument and a means to achieve competitive advantage. Corporate reputation is considered a key variable in improving the organization's attractiveness and its capacity for retention of both clients and investors. Organizations should consider the transmission of a positive image as an essential pre-condition for establishing a commercial relationship with target groups.

In the education realm, there is a growing recognition among academics and educational practitioners that a school's reputation is becoming increasingly important to stakeholders for both private and public school managers.

In a nutshell, good branding result to: enhanced recognition and reliability, builds a professional image and trust, emotional connection with the audience, drives growth, increases employee motivation, ensures market survival in times of stiff competition and crisis and attracts the right audience.

CHAPTER 2
BRANDING ELEMENTS

Branding elements are the key components that make up a cohesive and memorable brand identity. Greater knowledge of stakeholder perceptions about your organization will help to define the best reputational management platforms. Branding elements to measure corporate identity include:

1. Corporate design or visual identity referring to logos, uniforms, corporate colors, name, slogans, architecture and digital footprints.
2. Management and staff behavior expressed through corporate attitudes.
3. Corporate culture comprising of internal values, norms and beliefs, and attitudes.
4. Marketing communication referring to advertising, public relations and promotions.

DESIGN YOUR SIGNATURE LOOK

Corporate visual identities are the most powerful elements because of the physical and emotional appeal. Visuals are reflected through five main components namely: corporate name; symbol and/or logotype; typography; color; and slogan. It is also expressed through your signature architectural design on the ground and your digital profiles.

The identity elements are consistently applied using a guided style of logo, color, fonts and message tone. All internal stakeholders must be familiar with the rules of application. This guarantees consistent quality standards and contributes to the loyalty of customers. It should boost the loyalty of employees which is necessary for reputation building in educational institutions.

When a company needs to break from the past or be established in a particular market or adopt a new look after an acquisition; a change in the corporate name may also help in changing the corporate image. Visual identity components create emotional attachment. Educational organizations must be emotionally appealing which implies respectability, appreciation and trust.

Good corporate visual markers should at the bare minimum possess the following qualities for them to be effective: Be simple and clear to recognize, be symmetrical, appealing, uniformly and consistently applied in all corporate communication.

Braeburn School

An international school brand in Kenya.

Source: https://images.app.goo.gl/WnoGhs1uUzaJ11EE7

MODEL MANAGEMENT AND STAFF BEHAVIOUR

The component of behavior consists of management and employees attitudes. The aggregate of management style and staff behavior translates to a corporate culture. Employees' beliefs and attitudes should be quantified because reputation starts within the organization. Corporate reputation is not purely something for display to stakeholders at the annual general meetings. It is rooted in trust and is ethically shaped over time as reflected in the healthy attitudes employees have towards the organization and other stakeholders.

The quality of leadership affects school outcomes. There are five common aspects with leaders who get extraordinary things done: they model the way; inspire a shared vision; challenge the process; enable others to act; and encourage the heart. Educators should be appreciated so that they stay loyal, especially those who are exceptionally good and who go an extra mile. Teacher attrition rate is higher in schools that are poorly managed with low learner outcomes.

CHECK COMPANY TRADITIONS

Corporate Culture is a cocktail of the commonly held and relatively stable beliefs, attitudes and values that exist within the organization. Corporate culture in a school basically refers to the working and learning environment. Organizations must align their vision and mission to the needs of their stakeholders in order to build a strong brand and a solid reputation.

The best companies develop core values that impact on their company culture, brand, and business strategies, making them quite unique. A good workplace environment is safe and caring as core elements. People operate more like a community than an organization. All stakeholders feel good about the decisions made, they commit to the plan of action developed resulting in less absenteeism and the quality of work produced is of greater significance which produces a learning environment for students that is more conducive.

In a school, positive attitudes increase respectability. Positive attitudes always call for positive responses. Well-developed policies create an environment where educators and staff members enjoy their work. Organizational climate can be measured using the properties of the work environment, perceived directly or indirectly by the people who live and work in this environment. Potential learners look for a "great school" that has at its core an appealing culture and inspiring values.

HARNESS MARKETING COMMUNICATION TOOLS

Marketing communication strategies not only determines desired future states of the organization but also influence the formation of brand and corporate perceptions. The overall objective is to reach the target audience at the right time and in the most customer friendly manner. The firm attempts to generate a positive response in the target market by blending the four Ps marketing mix variables in an optimal manner in the form of product and services promotion.

The "Four Ps" marketing components are: Product, Price, Place, and Promotion.

- Product- Who are you as a company or school? What education products and services are you offering? What makes your brand unique?
- Price- Affordability depends on your niche market. What alternatives are offered by your competitors?
- Place- Who are your clients? Where are you located?
- Promotion- How do you contact your target audience?

Marketing may also take the form of a media advertisement campaign which is a planned attempt to influence public opinion behavior, attitudes and knowledge on behalf of some cause, person, institutions or topic, using different media over a specific period of time.

Schools should assign provision of education services a market value because it serves as a producer of educational products and services for its students. The school should also seek to attract donations of value; and knowledge-based services through grants and contract funders; and general support from the larger community. Educational institutes must shape a market offering that attracts investment, which comes from tuition and fees, grants and contracts, donors, state funding, and other activities.

In conclusion we can say that competition amongst schools is the solution to the problems of public schooling as much as we encourage competency based learning. Successful schools enjoy more frequent positive media coverage and donors.

A popular global school brand.

Source: https://images.app.goo.gl/qGMnUuAG3FfZ1e8X7

CHAPTER 3
SCHOOL BRANDING

School branding is the process of creating a set of elements that identify a school and recognize it from its competitors using different sets of reputation management tools. Marketing communication is an effective tool for strategic management of school brands and a means to influence their constituent stakeholders.

A super school brand must be dynamic to cope with the ever evolving global knowledge trends through embracing innovative approaches in education management. It must be well equipped to provide learners with the necessary 21st Century skills and purpose to produce well-rounded individuals. Ultimately, the super school must acquire a strong brand identity with a good reputation to appeal to the key stakeholders.

A corporation's reputation can influence the willingness of consumers to either provide or withhold support for a company and its products. A strong brand identity boosts reputation and shores up institutional success. A bad reputation in a school results in low morale for staff and students. Other stakeholders also often withhold their crucial support demanding for solid performance as a condition for continued support.

Schools must pay more attention to their corporate identity and deliberately respond to the interests of their key constituents of stakeholders to keep them satisfied. Experience confirms that an organization with a solid reputation earns the benefit of doubt from stakeholders even in times of crisis.

A loyal educator and a learner who identify themselves with the school can recommend the school to others as a nice place to work or receive education. Loyalty, respect, trust and appreciation are affected when educators and learners experience times of frustrations caused by insensitive educational policies that are unfriendly to educators' experiences and a curriculum that is also poorly designed, hence stressing learners.

It is a standard practice for schools to internally use school symbols, uniforms, and quality statements to express their core values and traditions, and service charters and strategic plans to guide management and staff behavior in an attempt at brand management. New students are taken through a rigorous form of indoctrination in the name of orientation with the aim of inculcating the schools' unique culture. New students also sign up to adhere to a certain code of conduct. Schools thus acquire and nurture unique cultures which identify them from the rest; thus serving as powerful identifying tools that propel them to excel in diverse fields and help to maintain high standards. Schools need to do more than this in marketing communication.

We can therefore say that schools that cut out an image of success become popular while those that are non-performing collapse losing their human and financial resources as well as goodwill from stakeholders until they are forced to either improve or close down. This applies to both private and public schools.

PILLARS OF A SUPER SCHOOL

1. A strong vision and mission with a clear purpose and direction.
2. A strong brand identity.
3. Excellent academic results.
4. Holistic development of talents and life skills.
5. Good stewardship in terms of management, following laid down rules, mentorship and role modeling support services.
6. Modern infrastructure with high levels of cleanliness, safety, access and adoption of modern digital technology.
7. Strong engagement and collaboration with the community.
8. Positive approval ratings by key stakeholders.

EFFECTS OF A GOOD SCHOOL REPUTATION

Stakeholders who enter into a relationship with an organization will be satisfied to the extent that their overall experience with the company has provided adequate value or benefits in relation to the resources that they have given up over the course of their relationship.

Below we discuss positive actions and attitudes from stakeholders that reflect satisfaction:

1. Attracting donations of value and grants from sponsors.
2. Attracting and retaining high caliber of students and parents which leads to growth of school enrollment.
3. Improved performance in exams and co-curricular activities.
4. Attracting partnerships and associates.
5. Positive comments from stakeholders.
6. High motivation for staff and students.
7. Pride and prestige in the school.
8. Feelings of safety and security which result in good conduct and stability.
9. Positive media coverage.

DETERMINE YOUR LEVEL OF COMPETITIVENESS

Schools like other companies compete by posing their best education products and services to their stakeholders. Depending on your location, competition might be stiff for both public and private schools. Stakeholders will most likely consider the following factors when choosing a great school:

- Academic Performance-What is your mean score in respect to your students' entry behavior and the category or class of your school?
- Discipline- Do a check on your stability, students and staff conduct.
- Management Behavior- Do you use innovative leadership styles?
- Motivation- Consider which incentives are in place to stimulate the performance of both staff and students.
- Facilities-What quality of infrastructure and learning resources are available?
- Co-curricular Activities-How broad is your talent and informal skills development strategy?
- Visual Appeal-Do you have physical and emotional connection with your stakeholders?

- Population-What is your level of establishment?
- Cost-Which target group can afford your education products and services?
- Access-where are you located?
- Curriculum Offered-How holistic is it?
- Safety- Is it a child friendly school?
- Sponsorship- What is your affiliation and funding model?
- Reputation-Do you appeal to your key constituents due to a targeted special achievement in a given discipline or social impact?
- Community Involvement-Connect with the people's needs.

Nairobi School Kenya Source: https://images.app.goo.gl/FfeNt5x6Sypfa9K68

Utumishi Boys Academy, Kenya.

Source:https://images.app.goo.gl/XNJgjafpUZu6UPSz8

MaryHill Girls Thika, Kenya

Source: https://images.app.goo.gl/4qyREKTKVYUj4JJP6

Some local super school brands in Kenya

CHAPTER 4
SCHOOL BRAND ASSETS

School brand assets are visual and emotional elements that represent a school identity to help communicate its values, mission and vision by creating positive feelings in students, parents, staff and other external stakeholders. Professor Berndt Schmitt of university of Colombia (https://business.columbia.ed) advises that a strong school brand must do the following:

1. They should provide a strong and visionary institutional leadership.
2. They set high expectations for excellent performance.
3. They have a well-defined and focused curriculum with tasks that are regularly reviewed and updated.
4. They promote high quality teaching by retaining skilled teachers.
5. They provide access to online teaching.
6. They encourage innovation, problem solving, self expression and a sense of freedom.

7. They embrace green initiative like supporting friendly, respectful and safe environmental interactions.
8. They promote healthy living campaigns.
9. They collaborate with parents and community in discussing matters like drug use, cyber bullying, and responsible use of social media and phones.
10. They use data to drive school decisions. Assess students' progress and adjust decisions.
11. They use student centered approaches to serve their needs.
12. The management promotes a strong sense of team work.
13. They clearly state the code of conduct. Hold individuals accountable for their actions and encourage positive behavior.
14. They build attractive well-designed buildings and well-maintained compounds and display artifacts and photos with school history.
15. They manage time well to enhance productivity.
16. They promote co-curricular activities to enhance mental and physical health, and talent development.

17. They promote responsible use of social media. Set rules and open a forum for safe use. Monitor platforms and address issues before they escalate.
18. They manage use of phones to avoid disruptions.
19. They promote continuous self-improvement; encourage innovation, self-appraisal and seeking feedback.
20. They maintain clean and hygienic facilities. Dirt is a big put off for all!

STRATEGIC BRAND TOOLS

These are purposefully selected designs and actions used to build and manage a brand. The key ones are:

1. Visual appeal

   Appealing physical symbols serve as powerful non-verbal messages for your school. The visual components include:

   Logo- It is a creative combination of symbols, names, colors and texts to represent your school identity.

   Corporate Theme Colors -Choose colors that represent you and which reflect your values.

   Special Typography-How do you want your texts to appear?

Pictorial Symbols- An image used to represent your core values.

Regalia-This refers to a collection of your official clothing or uniform, symbolic badges and ceremonial items. This includes school flag, insignia, trophies and mace.

The above components are consistently applied or displayed on school uniform, movable properties, buildings, compound and digital platforms.

Logo of Alliance Girls'/ Boys /Starehe Boys in Kenya.

Source:https://ekitabublog.wordpress.com/digital-leaders/secondary-high-schools

2. School Names-The official name and pet name of the school can carry some meaning for the stakeholders. A good or bad reputation can build around a name over time.

3. Design and Architecture- Your infrastructure designs can either be fixed or mobile. School buildings may have unique shapes, statues, paintings or inscribed patterns. Landscaping, fences and school gates also may have a

special significance and emotional attachment. Mobile infrastructure should also bring out your identity.

4. Branded Items- Pens, books, diaries, letter heads, calendars, cups, umbrellas and other school items carry a special emotional effect on the stakeholders.
5. Online and Digital Markers- How do you appear online in your websites, blogs, podcasts and social media. Professionally manage digital platforms for effect.
6. Print and audio-visual Identity- Radio and television can be used to reach out to your clientele. If need be, newspapers, magazines and brochures can be used to market the school.
7. Corporate Endorsement- Invite partners and associates with good reputations. They can be prominent people and high value institutions to help raise the profile of your school.
8. Corporate social responsibility programs- Participate in community events such as eg. Tree planting, blood donation events etc.
9. Organize School Events- They may include; prize giving day, sports day, careers day, fun days, parents open days, prayer days etc.

10. Manage performance in academics and co-curricular activities.
11. Manage staff and students attitudes through agreed school policies, code of conduct and school rules.
12. Manage access and affordability to be competitive depending on your niche market.
13. Effective management of communication and marketing.
14. Craft quality school statements which include: motto, vision, mission, core values, and service charter and strategic plan.
15. Highlight valued school traditions and history. Tell your school story in the best way possible.
16. Involve the school community in management when necessary.
17. Engage alumni ambassadors in school promotions.

BRANDING MISTAKES

1. You have no defined target audience hence no clarity on messaging.
2. Lack of consistency in messaging.
3. Frustrations when applying brand assets. Make it easy and friendly to use.
4. No clarity on what makes your school special.

5. Not sharing your story yourself thus leaving others to tell it. Tell your history, mission and values. Create a story or rallying call with an emotional connection to the audience eg. Moving forward together, changing lives.
6. Not show casing the people behind your success. Feature your key people to share in the glory of your achievements.

CHAPTER 5
RE-BRANDING YOUR SCHOOL

Re-branding is the process of changing a corporate image by overhauling or updating its brand elements to change the perceptions of stakeholders motivated by the need to break away from a negative past or in a spirited attempt to cope with emerging competitive environment. A good branding strategy in a school attracts the right students and supportive families.

A workplace environment that is conducive for effective learning in a school comprises the following key components: a physical environment that is welcoming; a social environment that promotes communication and interaction among stakeholders; an effective environment that promotes a sense of belonging and self-growth; and an academic environment that promotes learning and self-fulfillment.

Having discussed the benefits of branding, brand assets, brand elements and strategic brand tools; it is now time to re-brand our schools.

For easy demonstration, we first look at a step by step process:

1. Define Your School Purpose. Look for words that express what your school does and why

you do it. Reach out to parents, students and staff to find out their expectations.

2. Develop Your Brand Promise-It is your internal expression of your intent. What your customers should expect. One sentence of intent which is inspiring e.g.' We will create an environment that puts the students at the center of their learning, nurture curiosity and encourage students to achieve all-round learning and become independent creative thinkers.'

3. Create a Tagline-This is a power line for marketing and messaging e.g. Flower Academy: Learning for Life.

4. Establish Your Brand Identity-After crafting your purpose, promise and a tagline you have already shaped an identity. Express it verbally and visually through logo, color, typography, symbol and voice on social media, podcasts, print and website.

5. Establish Strong Brand Rules for consistent Application- The brand ambassadors should have unhindered but controlled access to brand assets.

6. Roll Out- Apply on signage, stationery, newsletter, uniforms, mascots, email headers and digital platforms.

5Ps BRAND PILLARS

Reflect on the following five pillars in the process of building your brand identity:

- **P**urpose-What vision drives your organization.
- **P**erception-How do customers think and feel about you.
- **P**ersonality- How do you speak to your customers, employees and work place culture that exists?
- **P**osition- What is your level of competitiveness.
- **P**romotion-How do you connect with your customers?

BRANDING TEMPLATE

A simple and standardized four stage instrument below can be used for brand construction as a template:

a. Investigate/Research- Do a SWOT and PESTLE analysis. Collect relevant data on your company history, target audience and competitors. Focus on both internal and external school environments and all stakeholders.

b. Analysis and Recommendation- Interpret data and draw conclusions. Determine your brand voice and personality. Write your brand story.

c. Developing the identity- Use the information collected to create an identity. Design your brand assets.

d. Launch – Implement the designed identity assets components.

THE 5Cs IN CRAFTING BRAND IDENTITIES

Your branding efforts will capture the attention of your target audience and make a strong statement and remain memorable if you apply the following 5cs:

Clarity - Use clear messaging tone.

Consistency- Applies uniformly across all brand touch points.

Content - Craft creative and quality brand assets.

Connection- Have an emotional bond.

Confidence- Believe in your brand and encourage loyalty.

SELF EVALUATION AND APPRAISSALS

Organizations should have the capacity to measure how their constituents perceive them, respond effectively to their feedback and appreciate the different dynamics of their environmental surroundings and learn what their constituents want and expect from them.

Measure the strength of your brand regularly to ensure that you maintain a positive brand score. You can use the following monitoring tools to maintain and calibrate your standards:

1. Strategic Plan- rate of execution of designated milestones.
2. Bench Marking and Annual Targets-Ensure you achieve set goals and borrow best practice from the best.
3. Exam Results- Analyze results regularly.
4. Policy Manuals - Guide on practice and ensure they are followed.
5. Performance Appraisals on Staff- Do assessments periodically.
6. Participating in Public Relations Events- This will help to get immediate feedback.
7. Customer Service Charters - Declare your service terms to your clients and follow them.
8. Daily or Weekly Performance Boards- Serve as reminders in the short term.
9. Code of Conduct and school Rules-Enforce agreed rules to create e harmony.
10. Motivation- Periodic performance awards serve to stimulate performance.

11. Feedback- Community engagement platforms provide channels for direct feedback.
12. Standards assessment and inspection reports- The respective government departments should regularly check on quality.
13. Digital search engines- analyze brand, queries, track customer reviews and ratings.
14. Media effects-Monitor mainstream media coverage and online appearances and number of mentions.
15. Research- Sponsor research findings on specific areas.

CHAPTER 6
THE WORLD TOP SCHOOL BRANDS

This chapter explores on specific logos, designs and other unique attributes that make a given school a reputable brand. We shall sample some top tier schools from over twelve countries in different regions of the world for purposes of comparision. The overall objective is to engage in a comparative study to identify common outstanding features in key schools that are geograghically spread out. Welcome so that we learn together the best practices from the best schools in the world.

1. St. Paul's School Sao Paulo,Brazil.

Motto: 'Esse Quam Videri'

Latin for – To be, Rather than to Seem.

Strengths

A. -It was founded in 1926.

B. -It is known for outstanding academic performance.

C. -Its graduates are admitted into world class universities.

D. -It has a strong co-curricullar program and offers an international academic curriculum.

CORE VALUES

-Kindness

-Resilience

-Inclusion

-Responsibility

-Adventure

-Aspiration

Picture: youtube.com/watch?v=guggfuf

Logo: fundacaostpauls.orf.br/a...

2. Robert College in Instabul Turkey

Motto: "Virtute et Literis"

Latin for –With Charater and Learning

Strengths

A. -It was founded in 1863 in Instabul and lies on a 65-acre campus.

B. -It has produced most of Turkish national elite.

C. It is extremely competitve with rigorous entry demands.

Picture: website.robcol.k12.tr/en... logo: rcaa.org/membership/rca...

3. Nada High School in Japan

Motto: Maximum Efficiency,Mutual welfare and Benefit.

The school has no official logo but it bases its identity on the above school philosophy and motto .

Strengths

A. It produces a high number of students joining Tokyo and Kyoto universities.

B. It is known to produce Olympiad medalists in prime subjects.

C. Their exams focus on problem-solving and logic.

CORE VALUES

-Respect

-Discipline

-Honesty

-Creativity

- Coperation

-Caring

-Fairness

-Excellence

Picture: en.wikipedia.org/wiki/na

4. **King'S College Budo,Uganda**

Motto: Gakyali (Luganda)

English meaning: So little done, so much more to do.

Strengths

A. A top tier school in Uganda which does well in national exams.

B. It has a high profile alumni.

C. It emphasis on character development,leadership,discipline and christian values.

D. It has a culture of excellence in debate,sports,sciences and music.

CORE VALUES

- Fear of God (Psalm 111:10)

- -Academic Excellence(Daniel 6:3-4)
- -Bravery for the truth (Daniel 3:16-18).
- Integrity(Psalm 25:21).
- Team work and Networking
- Respect for Self,Others,and Property(Mark 12:31)

Picture: schoolsuganda.com/school… Logo: seeklogo.com/vector-logo…

5. Moscow School 57, Russia

-It does not have an official school motto.

-School culture is guided by an informal but powerful educational philosophy.

-Unofficial guiding principle is:

"Learning is hard, but interesting"

Strengths

A. Its philosophy emphasize on the spirit of intellectual challenge and joy of discovery.

B. It focuses on critical thinking especially in Math and Sciences.

C. Learners are encouraged to take charge of their own learning and be original.

D. It uses seminar-style learning which encourages dialogue between teachers and students.

CORE VALUES

-Intellectual Curiosity & Independent Thinking

-Academic Excellence

-Integrity and Respect

-Rigorous Learning

-Talent Development and leadership

Logo: Ru.wikipedia.org/wiki/%d…
Picture:yandex.com/maps/org/mosc….

6. Shanghai High School China

Motto: Aspiration,Talent, Service to the Nation

Strengths

A. -It was founded in 1865 in Xuhui District in Shanghai.

B. It is known for producing high profile alumni.

C. -It blends traditional Gaokao excellence /Japan national exam with global curriculum innovations.

CORE VALUES

-Respecting international standards while preserving chinese characteristics.-

-Serving as a model window for East-west cultural exchange.

-Cultivating global-minded yet Chinese-rooted internal talents.

Logo: imagbin.com/png/8e2vhegr/...
picture: en.wikipedia.org/wiki/sh...

7. The Doon School Dehradun, India

Motto: Knowledge Our Light

Strengths

A. A private school founded in 1935 located in Dehran, Uttarrakhand lying on a 70 –acres campus with excellent facilities.

B. It is known for outstanding results with high university placements in global universities.

C. It is reputed to be 'The Eton of India.'

D. It has a high profile alumni in India.

E. It offers a broad curriculum in: Corporate, academic excellence,leadership, sports,drama and environmental stewardship.

CORE VALUES

-Excellence

-Integrity

-Leadership

-Service

-Respect for diversity

-Environmental Stewardship

-Creativity and Innovation

-Global Citizenship

THE DOON SCHOOL

Picture: schoolsofdehradun.com/sc..

Logo: en.wikipedia.org/wiki/th

8. St.John'S College ,South Africa

Motto: "Lux, Vita, Caritas "

English meaning: "Light,Life,Love"

Strengths

A. -It is located in Johannesburg in South Africa.
B. It is ranked among the best schools in South Africa offering Cambridge and A-levels exams.
C. -It is deep rooted in Aglican christian values.
D. -The alumni profile is rich and it basks in academic glory.

CORE VALUES

-Religious Discipline

-Academic excellence

-Goodwill or Service

Picture: lekkeslaap.co.za/attract…

Logo: x.com/stjohns-college

9. Chrisland High School, Nigeria

Motto: Show Forth the Light

Strengths

A. It is located in Lagos Nigeria and was founded in 1977.

B. It boosts of modern architectural style and consistently high performance.

C. It has earned top global rankings in IGCSE in Agriculture and Law studies.

CORE VALUES

-Discipline

-Integrity

-Professionalism

-Love

-Excellence

Picture: chrislandschools.co/chr..

Logo: schoolsnigeria.wordpress...

10. British International School Cairo,Egypt

Motto:Lead the way

Strengths

A. It is a private school founded in 1976 offering IGCSE and A-level curiculum.

B. It has recorded high admissions to world class universities with students from 50+ different nationalities.

CORE VALUES

-Academic excellence

-Independent learning

-Global Citizenship

-Integrity &Responsibility

-Personal Growth

-Supportive & Discipline Community

THE BRITISH
INTERNATIONAL
SCHOOL, CAIRO

Logo: bisc.edu.eg/about-bisc-2…

Picture: bsmeu15.weebly.co/briti…

11. Phillip's Exeter Academy , USA

Motto: "Non Sibi"

English meaning: Not for Oneself.

The school hymn is titled The Hymn of Phillips Exeter, a modern ceremonial intended to reflect Exeter's values of community, service and tradition.

Strengths

A. It is a private school founded in 1781 in New Hampshire with world class facilities and huge financial resources of over $1.3 billion.

B. It records high admissions into Ivy League universities.

C. It is ranked as number one US preparatory school with a rich alumni profile.

D. It offers exceptional curriculum using Harkness method/ student led roundtable discussions.

CORE VALUES

-Knowledge & Goodness

-academic Excellence

-Youth from Every Quarter

-Youth Is the Important Period

-Non Sibi (Not oneself)

Picture:exeter.edu/about/our-cam

Logo:exeter.epu/aponf/onl-cam

12. Eton College ,England

Motto: Floreat Etona

English meaning: Let Eton Flourish.

It has another motto: Esto Perpetua- Be Eternal.

The official school anthem of Etton College is the Latin song Carmen Etonense a treasured part of Etonian tradition.

Strengths

A. It is reputed to be among the best schools world wide with a high profile alumni .

B. It has rich traditions ,uniforms and royal connections.

C. It focuses on: leadership development,public speaking,debate and critical thinking.

CORE VALUES

-Academic Excellence & Intellectual Curiosity

-Personal Character & Integrity

-Autonomy with accountability

-Balance Development (Co-curriculum)

- Community & Service

Logo: en.wikipedia.org/wiki/et..

Picture: warrenpropertymatters.on

SAMPLES OF SCHOOL REGALIA AND DIGITAL PROFILES

It is worth noting that most established schools have a cache of accessories used to promote their school culture.

Sample School Flags

Sources: shopandoverpa.com/proc...

Dribble.com/shots/23615...'

Sample School Maces

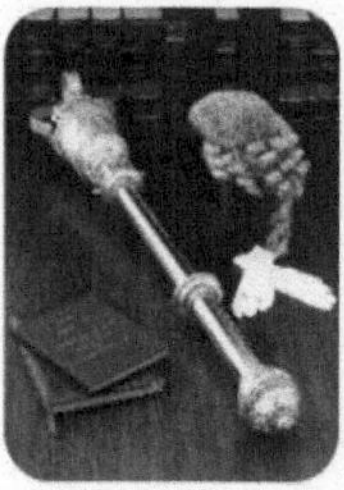
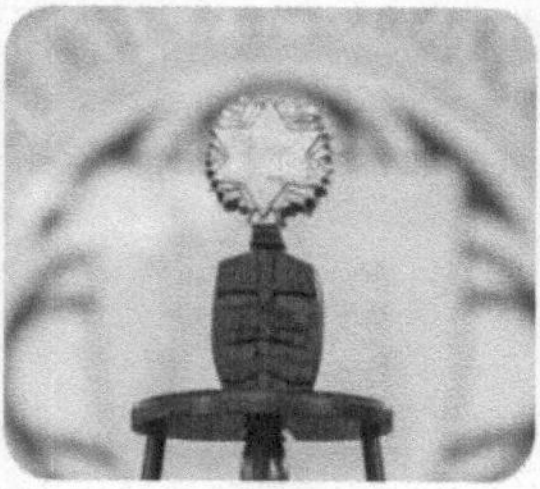

Sources: en.wikipedia.or/wiki/ce...

Sample Honour Board

Source:: Au.pinterest.com/pin/ab-...

Sample Trophy Board

Source:Statelinepubs.com/swea-h...

Samples of School Statues

Sources:randolprose.com/proct...

School Uniform

Source:etoncollege.com/about-us...

SAMPLE SCHOOL ANTHEM

Green hill Academy School Anthem

Title: "O Greenhill, Strong and true"

Verse 1

O Greenhill, Strong and true you stand,

A guiding light across the land.

With minds that grow and hearts that care,

We learn, we lead, we dare, to dream,

Together strong, a shining team.

Verses 2

With discipline and voices clear,

We walk with courage, free from fear.

Integrity our guiding flame,'

We lift on high your noble name.

Bridge

From every dawn to setting sun,

Your lessons shape us, every one.

We pledge our hearts, our minds, our will,

To honor you, dear Greenhill still.

Final chorus (slow and strong)

Greenhill, Greenhill, ever true,

Our lives are brighter thanks to you.

With honor, hope and service done-

We shine as many, rise as one.

Source: Wikipedia Greenhill School (Addison, Texas).

School Websites

Source: Muffingroup.com/blog/sch...

Source:campussprespress.com/your-com..

COMMON FEATURES OF THE TOP SCHOOL BRANDS ABOVE

1. They record sterling performances in exams which help students to secure placement in premium colleges and universities.
2. They have a rich legacy of alumni who have made great impact in their societies.
3. They offer a broad based curriculum with emphasis on talent development, nurturing of life skills with deeply entrenched school traditions.
4. They adopt innovative learning methods and harness technology.
5. They take keen interest in environmental stewardship and champion community interests.
6. They have and attract immense learning resources from key stakeholders.
7. They have well maintained modern facilities.
8. They use student centered learning approaches.
9. Their Motto, logos and designs aim to inspire and connect emotionally with key stakeholders.

10. They possess a repertoire of artifacts and slogans that helps to build the school's history and identity.

REFERENCES

1. Anderson, E. W., Claes F., and Donald R. L. (1994), "Customer Satisfaction, Market Share, and Profitability: Findings from Sweden." Journal of Marketing,58 (3), 53.
2. Donaldson, T. &. Preston, L. E. (1995), "The Stakeholder Theory of the Corporation: Concepts, Evidence, and Implications."Academy of Management Review, 20 (1), 65-91.
3. Freeman, R.E. (1984). Strategic management: A stakeholder approach. N Y: Basic Books.
4. Gregory, A. (2007). Involving stakeholders in developing corporate brands: the communication dimension. Journal of Marketing Management, 23 (1-2), 59-73.
5. Grunig, J. E. & Hunt, T (1984).Managing Public Relations. New York: Holt, Rinehart and Winston.
6. Kitchen P J and Schultz D E(2000). Raising the Corporate Umbrella: Corporate Communications in the 21st century (2002), Corporate Reputation Review, Vol 5 Numbers 2 & 3, pp266-268, Henry Stewart Publications.
7. Melewar, T. C. & Jenkins, D. E., (2000a).Defining corporate identity – the search for a holistic model. Advanced Issues in Marketing. Warwick Business School.
8. Nizar S., Norizan M. K & Heung-Ja H. (2006).The effect of corporate branding dimensions on consumers' product evaluation: A cross-cultural analysis. European Journal of Marketing Vol. 40 No. 7/8, 2006 pp. 825-845 q

9. Ngugi. P.K (2016).Assessing the Impact of strategic communication management on stakeholders in public schools in Kenya. IJSR Volume 1 Oct1, 2016.
10. Olins, W., (1989).Corporate identity: Making business strategy visible through design. London: Thames and Hudson.

This book aims at raising awareness of school leaders on how to manage their school brands and turn them into Super Schools. As you engage with stakeholders, a school may acquire a good reputation or a bad reputation. A good reputation will attract stakeholder support enabling that school to have: high students enrolment, high mean scores, modern infrastructure, endowment in learning resources, capacity for talent mobilization and development, motivated staff and students, happy external stakeholders, and stability in terms of students conduct and discipline. Bad reputations stifle school growth absolutely. Re-branding will help you to bounce back to life!

AUTHOR PROFILE

Ngugi P.K is a graduate in Master of Science in Mass communication from JKUAT, Kenya (2016); BED arts degree-MOI University (1999); Diploma in Education-KEMI (2017) and CICT-KASNEB (2011) SECT 1. He has a wide range of experience in teaching and education management. He is also a researcher in education matters, life skills and an author of several books and journals with a bias on topics related to youth development and empowerment.